The Road to Financial Freedom: Investing for a Better Tomorrow

<u>Table of Contents:</u>

Chapter 20: Protecting Yourself from Financial Scams and Fraud

Closing Thoughts

<u>Disclaimer:</u>

The information contained in this book is for informational purposes only and is not intended to be a substitute for professional financial or tax advice. The tax laws are constantly changing and vary based on individual circumstances/locations. Therefore, the accuracy of the information contained in this book cannot be guaranteed. Always seek the advice of a qualified financial or tax professional regarding your financial situation. This book does not provide financial, legal, or tax advice and the author/publisher assumes no responsibility for any actions or inactions taken by the reader. Use the information in this book at your own risk.

<u>About the Author:</u>

My name is Nathan, I wanted to start by saying thanks again for checking out this book. I worked hard on this and I appreciate you taking the time to check it out. I wanted to take a minute to give you some information about myself. I am currently 25 years old and I was born in Newfoundland but I currently live in Alberta and this is where I've spent most of my life. I have a huge passion for investing and all things related to finance. I have a lovely spouse who is extremely supportive of anything I want to do and I appreciate her so much for all the help and support she gives. I wanted to take a second to thank her for everything, we have a beautiful son at the time of writing he is just over 14 months old. I currently run a Twitter (X) account for teaching people about investing plus providing support and motivation about all things investing. My main goal is to help anyone I can with support and advice. Some of my biggest motivators in my daily life include my spouse, my parents, and my son. When it comes to investing my motivation stems from the famous investor John C. Bogle, and the motivational speakers Les Brown, Tony Robbins, and David Goggins.

Opening:

Welcome to the world of investing! My name is Nathan, known to most as "DividendKingTSX" on Twitter(X) and Blossom Social, I'm thrilled to have you with me on this journey of discovery. Investing is a critical component of financial literacy, and I'm honored that you've chosen to embark on this learning experience with me. Whether you're brand new to the subject, or you already have some experience, this book is designed to help you understand the fundamentals of investing, including the psychology behind it. The world of investing can be a complex and daunting place, but I'm here to try and simplify it for you and make it accessible to everyone.

Investing is not just about numbers and financial ratios, it's also about the understanding of your own emotions and biases, and how they can impact your investment decisions. This is why I want to touch on the psychology of investing and help you understand how to stay level-headed, even in the face of market volatility.

My goal is to make investing a less intimidating and more accessible topic, and I hope that you find this book to be a helpful and engaging resource. I'm confident that by the end of it, you'll have a solid understanding of the basics of investing, and be equipped with the tools you need to start making informed decisions. So without further ado, let's dive right into this exciting world of investing!

Chapter 1:

Introduction to Investing & Motivation for Investing

Investing can be a powerful tool for helping you accumulate wealth and achieve your long-term financial goals. For example, I am investing in dividend-paying stocks/ETFs to replace the income I receive from my 9-5 with a passive source. I know a lot of people find the idea of investing to be intimidating, and I am hoping I can help out a little with this. Whether you're just getting started or if you have some experience, understanding the basics of investing is vital for becoming a successful investor.

In this section of the book, we'll discuss what investing is and what makes it so important. We will also touch on some basic concepts and terms that you should learn to fully understand the world of investing.

What is investing?

Investing is the process of using money to purchase different assets to generate a return or grow your income over time. It's important to have diversity in your investment portfolio, one way to achieve this is by understanding the different types of assets available to invest in. These include options like stocks, bonds, mutual funds, real estate, and alternative investments. Each type of asset has unique characteristics regarding risk and potential returns.

Why is investing important?

Investing plays a crucial role in financial planning, it has several benefits:

- Firstly, it enables you to watch your money increase over time, particularly for long-term objectives like retirement or a child's education. I started investing around the age of 21 but started taking it more seriously when I was closer to 24. Since I began to invest regularly, watching my money grow and make more money has been like magic.
- Secondly, it protects your money from losing purchasing power to inflation. If the last few years showed us anything, its inflation can rise fast, making it harder to save if you are only holding cash.
- Lastly, by diversifying your income streams through investing, you can be less dependent

on a single source of income to achieve your financial goals. I always want to try to gain more income streams, having one is too close to none!

Basic concepts and terminology:

When first starting with investing, it is important to familiarise yourself with some key terms and concepts to make informed investment choices, it's easy to get overwhelmed so I'll try to break it down to the key terms.

Here are a few of the most important ones:

- ETF: An ETF is an investment fund. ETFs hold a collection of assets, like stocks, bonds, commodities, or maybe a combination of these, they are designed to track the performance of a market index. More on them in a later chapter.
- Stock: A stock or share, is a unit of ownership of a company. By buying a stock, you become a part-owner of that company and have a claim on a portion of its profits, represented by dividends.
- Risk: The possibility of an investment losing value. Generally, investments with higher potential returns come with a higher level of

risk and vice versa. It is important to have a good understanding of your risk level before investing any money.

- Return: The profit/loss from an investment. Normally a percentage. Returns can come in the form of interest, dividends, or stock price appreciation.
- Dividend: The portions of earnings some companies pay to their shareholders. Dividends are normally received quarterly, occasionally a few stocks and ETFs pay them monthly.
- Diversification: A strategy of investing in a variety of different assets to reduce the overall risk of your portfolio.

Now that you have a basic understanding of what investing is and why it is essential, you're ready to start exploring the different types of investment strategies and assets that are available to you. Coming up you'll be learning about risk, risk management, and the psychology behind investing.

Investing is a topic that can seem daunting and overwhelming to many people, but it is a powerful tool that can help you achieve your financial goals. In this chapter, we will delve deeper into the various motivators for investing and how to develop clear financial goals to help you stay focused and achieve your investment objectives.

One of the most obvious motivators for investing is the potential for wealth creation over time. By investing your money, you can achieve higher returns than what you would typically get from a savings account. This means you can grow your wealth, protect it against inflation, and potentially achieve financial independence. The idea of being in control of your financial future and being able to live on your terms is a powerful motivator for many people.

But investing is not just about money; it's also about control and empowerment. By taking an active role in your financial future and investing, you are making informed decisions that will shape your life. Investing can also provide a sense of satisfaction, fulfillment, and personal accomplishment. Some people find that investing gives them a sense of purpose and helps them stay motivated to achieve their financial goals.

In addition to financial gain and personal fulfillment, investing can also serve as a means of providing for future generations. For instance, the desire to teach your children everything you know and set them up for success is a strong motivator for many parents. By investing wisely, you can build wealth that will benefit your children and grandchildren for years to come.

Having clear financial goals is crucial when it comes to investing. When you have a well-defined objective, it becomes easier to stay focused and motivated on your investing journey. Additionally, by setting goals, you can develop a plan to reach them and make better investment decisions. This can involve diversifying your portfolio and working with a financial advisor to help you achieve your goals.

It's important to note that what motivates one person may not be the same for another. Understanding your motivations and having clear financial goals, along with a well-defined plan, can help you stay motivated and focused on achieving your investment objectives. But it's also important to remember that investing carries risks, and that's why it's important to seek the advice of professionals, including a tax professional and a financial advisor, to help you make informed decisions.

Furthermore, it's essential to keep in mind that tax laws change, and your financial situation is unique to you. Therefore, the information in this book is for informational purposes only and not tax or financial advice. Seek the advice of professionals to ensure that you receive advice specific to your financial situation. We talk more about taxes in a later portion of the book.

Investing is a vast and complex subject that offers endless possibilities for growing wealth and achieving financial goals. However, the abundance of investment options available can be daunting for investors, especially those who are just starting. Choosing the right type of asset to invest in requires an understanding of the risks and potential returns associated with each investment option. In this next section, we'll explore some of the more common types of investments and what they have to offer.

Stock Market Investing:

One of the more popular forms of investing is buying stocks, or shares, of different publicly traded companies. When you buy shares of a company, you are a part owner of the company, this is very important as it's easy to get caught up in the excitement and you may forget that you're not just buying a symbol and there is a company behind that ticker, we talk about this more in a later chapter. Another thing to consider is as a shareholder you can be entitled to a share of the company's profits in the form of dividends more on this in a future chapter. The value of the stock you bought can also increase over time if the company performs well, and if the world isn't in a global downturn or event providing the potential for capital appreciation on top of the dividends. With how accessible the stock market is to the average person nowadays, I believe everyone should be investing, most brokerages are either free or very cheap!

Real Estate Investing:

Another popular form of investing is real estate. Investing in real estate can be done by buying property, renting it out, and collecting rental income. Something to keep in mind is some risks come along with this, as in you could have bad tenants who are either late on paying or damaging the property. It is important to do proper background checks on someone you'd be interested in renting to. This is one of my longer-term goals, I would like to have a few properties rented out. Another thing about real estate is it also has the possibility for capital appreciation over time as the value of the property increases. Additionally, one of the easier ways to dip your toes into real estate investing is to invest in real estate investment trusts, or REITs for short, which are companies that own/operate real estate properties taking the work out of your hands.

Bond Investing:

Bonds are debt securities issued by companies or governments that pay interest to the holders. They are considered a more conservative investment in comparison to stocks and are generally considered to be less risky. Bonds can help you provide a steady stream of income and can be used as a way to diversify your portfolio.

Mutual Fund Investing:

Mutual funds are also another popular investment choice. Mutual funds are a type of investment vehicle that takes money from multiple different investors and buys a diversified portfolio of stocks/bonds or other securities. Those portfolios are then watched and managed by professional money managers who offer investors an easy way to participate in the stock market without having to pick and choose an individual asset.

Alternative Investing:

Alternative investments would be considered to be investments that are anything but traditional investments such as stocks, bonds, or cash. These kinds of investments can include hedge funds, private equity, and derivatives. Alternative investments can be more complex and sometimes that means less liquid than traditional investments, this also means they can often carry higher risk.

In summary, there are many different types of investing to choose from, each comes with its own set of risks or potential returns. Understanding the differences between them can help you make more informed investment decisions and build a diversified investment portfolio that aligns with your financial goals and risk tolerance.

To summarise, investing can provide both financial and non-financial motivation, and having clear financial goals, along with a well-defined plan, is crucial for staying motivated and achieving your investment objectives. By being aware of the risks and seeking professional advice, you can develop an investment strategy that works for you and helps you achieve your financial goals. Investing can also serve as a means of providing for future generations and passing on your wealth to your loved ones,

which can be a significant motivator for many
people.

Chapter 2:

The Psychology of Investing

Investing is not only about numbers; it's also about the emotions and psychology of the investor. The way that we feel and think about money, risk, and investing can have a huge impact on our investment decisions, ultimately affecting our financial well-being. In this section, we are going to explore the emotional and psychological factors that can influence someone's investment decisions and examine how they could affect our performance as investors.

Emotions with investing:

Emotions unfortunately can play a significant role in investment decisions. Some emotions such as greed, fear, and hope could cause you to make bad investment decisions. The fear of losing money can make an investor sell stocks too early, leading to missed potential gains. Greed can lead an investor to buy risky assets, hoping for quick gains. Hope is also another powerful emotion while investing, as it could cause an investor to hold on to a losing investment for too long, instead of limiting their losses by selling the asset.

Investing isn't just about numbers or statistics, it is important to understand and manage your biases and emotions. As we are only humans, we are known for making emotional decisions that can more often than not lead to poor investment choices. This illustrates why it's important for you to have a clear understanding and picture of your psychology and how it could affect your investment decisions now and in the future.

A common emotional bias is fear. Fear of losing money is a huge reason an investor may sell their investments at the wrong time, or early, missing out on potential gains. This is normally referred to as the "fear of missing out" or "FOMO" and it causes investors to make fast and most of the time poor decisions based on the fear of missing out on any potential profits there "may" be. A way you can combat this bias is to have a long-term investment plan and stick to it, even when there are market downturns. Most new investors will experience this at least once for me. When I first started I was buying a biotech stock strictly because the price ran up so much the week before, and I thought it would keep going. I know now this is a dangerous emotion and most of the time it only leads to losses.

Also, investors should spend more time focusing on the possible returns of an investment, instead of the potential losses. It's important to not forget short-term market fluctuations are normal and that over time, the market tends to go up. Another emotional bias is greed. Greed can cause investors to make decisions without much thought, as in buying high and then selling low. This could also be referred to as "chasing returns" and it's a classic mistake that many investors make when they see an investment that has had a recent period of high returns. I knew early on not to be greedy when it comes to investing, but most don't learn until they've made the mistake.

To combat this bias, investors should have a clear understanding of their risk tolerance and stick to the investment plan that they have laid out. Additionally, investors shouldn't ever chase hot stocks or try to time the market, this often ends poorly. Instead, they should focus on buying the undervalued assets at the time that have the potential for long-term growth/dividend increases over time. It's also really important to understand the impact of emotions on your investment decisions and why it is so important to control them. For example, more often than not, feelings of regret can cause investors to hold on to losing investments for too long, rather than cutting their losses earlier on. This is known as "anchoring" and it's another common bias that investors may fall into when they are too attached to an investment. I'm guilty of this, at the time of writing I have a stock I'm down around 70% and am still holding when in reality I should've cut my losses early. I hold this stock as a reminder to be logical and not allow myself to repeat this mistake.

To avoid this, it's important to have a clear exit strategy for investments that are not performing well, this should be part of your investment plan. This means setting a target price or a stop-loss order that will trigger a sale if the investment reaches a certain value. There can be certain rules when it comes to this, but you should try and stick to this exit strategy, and your full investment plan so you don't fall victim to one of the above biases.

<u>Behavioural biases:</u>

Investors are also often misled by behavioral biases. These cognitive biases are often not conscious and cause any rational decision-making to disappear. Some of the more common biases are:

- **Overconfidence bias:** Investors who've gotten lucky before may tend to overestimate their abilities

to predict the future and make great investment
decisions, often not seeing the risks or potential
mistakes. This is common but can be very
dangerous for new investors who don't fully
understand what they are doing.

- **Anchoring bias:** Investors tend to rely too heavily
on the first piece of information they receive when
making an investment decision. This can be very
damaging to investors as they can be blinded by this
information and miss other problems.

- **Herding bias:** Investors who follow the crowd
and make investment choices based on what others
are doing rather than their research. Don't get
caught up in something you don't fully understand.
Don't buy a stock just because you keep seeing it on
social media, just because someone else is buying it
doesn't mean it's a good investment, always do
your research before purchasing anything.

Managing emotions and biases

Managing your emotions and biases is crucial for
making solid investment decisions. One of the best
ways to do this is by educating and practicing
self-awareness. By taking time to educate ourselves
on the basics of investing, we can make more
informed decisions and avoid common pitfalls. That
is my main goal with this book, to teach people and
help them understand the risks of emotional

investing. A way to manage your emotions and biases is by having an investment plan, but also sticking to it. A well-structured and thought-out investment plan or outline can help us stay grounded and focused on our long-term goals. It's also helpful to have a support system, this could be a financial advisor/mentor, or for me it's Twitter, to help provide a sense of accountability and or provide a different perspective on investment choices.

When making decisions regarding investments, it is essential to maintain objectivity and discipline. This is because investing requires financial decisions with long-term ramifications, and emotions can impair judgment, resulting in rash and ill-considered actions.

Investors can minimize the risk of impulsive or emotionally motivated choices by remaining disciplined and objective. This allows them to make informed decisions that are in line with their investment objectives. This can help make sure that decisions about investments are made on relevant data and information, not feelings like fear or greed.

In addition, adhering with discipline to a clearly defined investment strategy, even in the face of market volatility or short-term losses, can assist in avoiding rash decisions and guaranteeing the achievement of long-term investment objectives.

In summary, it is important to understand the psychology of investing so you can make sound investment decisions. Emotions and biases can sometimes cloud our judgment and then lead to poor investment decisions. By being aware and alert of our emotions or biases or by taking steps to manage them, we can become better investors and make more informed decisions.

Chapter 3:

Understanding & Managing the Risks of Investing

It is important to keep in mind that investing can come with a certain level of risk, as the value of your investment can and will fluctuate over time based on a variety of different factors. Some of the factors that can affect your investment value are market conditions, economic conditions, and company performance. It's important to understand these risks before investing and also to have a plan in place to manage the risk to the best of your ability.

Types of risk

One of the more significant risks of investing would be market fluctuations. If we look at the stock market, for example, it is known for being volatile, meaning stock prices can rise and fall dramatically over a short period. This means that the value of your investments can change rapidly, and you could potentially lose money if you're not ready for market downturns. One way to mitigate this risk is to consider diversifying your portfolio. You can do this by investing in a variety of different assets or industries. This way, if one specific area of the market is not performing well, other parts of your portfolio may balance out the potential losses, providing some level of protection against overall portfolio losses.

Another important thing the investor should consider is asset allocation. This is the mix of different kinds of investments inside of your portfolio, this can be stocks, bonds, or cash. It is important to remember each type of investment has its own unique risk and return characteristics, so it's critical to have a balance of different assets to help achieve your investment goals while doing the best to limit risk.

In addition to market asset allocation and fluctuations, investors should also think about the impact of taxes on the investments they make. Some investments could be tax-free or offer tax advantages. It's important to understand the tax implications of your investments and make decisions accordingly before making a purchase. I will not be talking about taxes in this book as it is different for everyone depending on your current situation. It is always recommended to consult an expert about taxes to get proper information.

Finally, almost just as important as the rest is to consider the cost of investing, this would be the management fees for ETFs or trading costs your broker might charge. These costs have the potential to eat into your returns over time, so it's important to be cautious of them when choosing your investment products.

In conclusion, investing can be and is a powerful tool for building wealth, but it's important to understand the risks involved so you can make informed decisions to manage the risks. By taking the time to consider factors such as market fluctuations, asset allocation, taxes, and costs, you can build a diversified portfolio that aligns with your investment goals and risk tolerance.

Risk is an intrinsic piece of investing, and understanding various kinds of risks and how to oversee them is essential for long-haul achievement. In this section, we will investigate six vital sorts of risks that financial backers ought to know about market risk, credit risk, inflation risk, liquidity risk, political risk, and operational risk.

Market Risk: Market risk alludes to the uncertainty related to the changes in the value of assets because of developments in the financial exchange. This can be relieved by diversifying across various sorts of resources, like bonds and stocks, as well as various geographical regions.

Credit Risk: Credit risk refers to the possibility that a borrower may default on a loan or bond, leading to a loss for the lender. This risk can be managed by investing in bonds with high credit ratings and by diversifying investments across different types of borrowers.

Inflation Risk: Inflation risk refers to the possibility that the purchasing power of money will decrease over time due to inflation. This risk can be managed by investing in assets that have the potential to increase in value faster than inflation, such as stocks and real estate.

Liquidity Risk: Liquidity risk refers to the possibility that an investor may not be able to sell their investments quickly enough to meet their financial needs. This risk can be managed by investing in highly liquid assets, such as exchange-traded funds and money market funds.

Political Risk: Political risk refers to the possibility that government actions or events may negatively impact investments. This can be mitigated by investing in politically stable countries and diversifying investments across different regions.

Operational Risk: Operational risk refers to the possibility of losses due to problems with internal systems, processes, and people. This risk can be managed by investing in companies with strong management teams and robust internal controls.

In conclusion, managing risk is an important aspect of investing, and understanding different types of risks and how to mitigate them can help investors make informed decisions. By considering market, credit, inflation, liquidity, political, and operational risks, investors can build a well-rounded investment portfolio that meets their financial goals.

Chapter 4:

Setting Investment Goals and creating a Custom Financial Plan

Creating a financial plan that is custom to you plus setting investment goals should be considered essential steps in becoming a successful investor. A financial plan is a document that can be as simple as your main goals and rules that you've laid out, or it can be as complex as you'd like. Some financial plans include your short-term and long-term goals and your current financial situation and they may also include the steps required to achieve them. It could also have your budget, your net worth, your cash flow, and your investment portfolio.

The distinction between medium-term and short-term goals can be quite significant when it comes to investing and financial planning. To develop an effective investment strategy that aligns with your overall financial goals, it is essential to comprehend the distinctions between the two types of goals.

Typically, short-term goals are those that will be accomplished within the next one to five years.

They are usually related to day-to-day expenses and short-term investments and are focused on immediate financial requirements. Purchasing a house, paying off credit card debt, or starting an emergency fund are all examples of short-term objectives.

On the other hand, medium-term goals are typically thought of as objectives that will be accomplished within the next six to ten years. They are frequently connected to investments and intermediate financial requirements that call for a little bit more perseverance and time to fulfill. Purchasing additional properties, starting a business, or creating a retirement fund are examples of medium-term objectives.

Once you have set your custom goals, you also need to have a strategy to help achieve them. This includes determining your risk tolerance which we've talked about in the last chapter. Also deciding on an asset allocation that aligns with your risk tolerance and goals, for example, my allocation is 80% ETFs and 20% Stocks at this time. Asset allocation is the process of splitting up your portfolio between different classes, such as stocks, ETFs, bonds, GICs, etc. Each asset class has its own unique risk and return characteristics, but by taking the time and effort to diversify your portfolio, you can reduce your overall risk. Below we will take a look at my short-term and medium-term goals.

My short-term goals: (1-5 years)

- Buy property end of 2024 or the start of 2025
- Continue to invest 80/20 split into ETFs/Stocks reinvest dividends
- Go to school
- Start side gigs/discover more passive income streams
- Keep an open mind to new investments

My medium-term goals: (6-10 years)

- Start using the dividends from my ETFs to accumulate more individual stocks for long-term holds
- Buy second & third properties depending on the market and if everything goes smoothly
- Start some sort of business/purchase business

Here are a few more key points for setting goals and plans:

A financial plan is reviewed and updated regularly:

Your financial plan must be reviewed and updated regularly as your objectives and circumstances shift. This will assist you in maintaining your progress toward your goals.

The significance of emergency funds:

An essential component of a financial plan is having an emergency fund. In times of uncertainty, this fund should be used to cover unexpected expenses and provide financial stability.

Consider professional assistance:

To assist you in developing and maintaining a comprehensive financial plan, think about consulting a professional or financial advisor. They can offer helpful advice and insights on a variety of topics, including retirement planning, tax planning, and investment options.

Research and education:

Investing and financial planning can be difficult, so it's important to keep up your education and investigate various investment options. To stay on course, keep up with changes in your circumstances and the market.

Flexibility:

Your financial plan must be adaptable, and your strategy must be modified as necessary. If you think your plan isn't working or if your goals have changed, don't be afraid to make adjustments.

Discipline and patience:

Finally, patience and discipline are necessary for successful financial planning and investing. Maintaining your course of action and avoiding emotional impulsiveness are essential. Keep in mind that investing is a long-term endeavor, and it may take some time to achieve your goals.

One of the most important aspects of investing is having a clear and well-defined budget. This means having a clear understanding of how much money you can afford to invest, as well as how you will track and monitor your investment spending. A budget can help you to make informed decisions about your investments and to avoid overspending or taking on too much risk.

To get started with setting your investment budget, you will need to determine your current income and expenses. This should include all sources of income, including your salary, rental income, and any other sources of income. You should also include all of your monthly expenses, such as housing, utilities, transportation, food, and entertainment.

Once you have an accurate understanding of your income and expenses, you can begin to determine how much money you have available to invest. A general rule of thumb is to invest between 10 to 20 percent of your income. However, the exact amount that you invest will depend on your financial situation, risk tolerance, and investment goals.

It is important to also consider the different types of investments that you will make, and how these investments will impact your budget. For example, if you invest in a stock, you may need to pay brokerage fees and taxes depending on the account, whereas if you invest in a mutual fund, you may be required to pay an annual management fee.

Once you have established your investment budget, you should create a system for tracking and monitoring your investment spending. This can be as simple as using a spreadsheet, or you may choose to use a more sophisticated tracking tool, such as a financial management software program.

Regardless of the method that you choose, it is important to regularly review and update your investment budget to ensure that it remains in line with your financial goals and that you are making the most of your investment dollars. You should also regularly review your investments to ensure that they are performing as expected and that they are aligned with your investment goals and risk tolerance.

In conclusion, creating a financial plan and setting investment goals are essential for becoming a successful investor. It is important to have a comprehensive understanding of your current financial situation, your short-term and long-term goals, and the steps you need to take to achieve them. Additionally, risk management and diversification are key elements for a successful investment strategy. It is also important to keep in mind that it is okay to change your goals and what you want in life, a lot of things can affect your goal-making decision and it is important not to rush this process.

Chapter 5:

Building and maintaining a Diversified Investment Portfolio

In this section of the book, we are going to talk about how putting your money into investments can help you achieve your financial objectives and build wealth over time. However, it can be challenging to choose the best investment strategy because there are so many options. This book's previous chapters have laid the groundwork for investment success. We've discussed how important it is to make a financial plan, set goals for investments, know your risk tolerance, and use asset allocation to diversify your portfolio. All of these ideas are necessary for creating an efficient investment strategy. In this chapter, we will discuss various investment strategies that can assist you in achieving your objectives.

It is essential to keep in mind that the strategy you select ought to be compatible with your investment objectives and overall financial plan. A more conservative investment strategy would be appropriate, for instance, if your primary objective is to generate income and preserve capital. On the other hand, if you want to build wealth over time, a more aggressive strategy could be better for you. It will be easier for you to choose the best investment strategy for you if you are familiar with your financial situation and investment objectives.

One of the most important ways to lessen the risk in your investment portfolio is to diversify your portfolio, this is a big reason I hold 80% ETFs and only a few individual stocks. This allows me to diversify in multiple markets with relatively little risk, which is a fundamental investment principle. By spreading your investments across a variety of asset classes, industries, and geographical regions, diversification works. Because the performance of one investment may not be indicative of the performance of the entire portfolio, this helps to reduce the risk associated with any one investment.

For instance, you would be taking on a significant amount of risk if you put all of your money into a single stock. When I first started investing, this was something I struggled with. I had over 90% of my portfolio tied up into one asset and lost around 60% of my portfolio's value because of one asset. Having your entire investment portfolio decline if that stock were to lose value isn't a nice feeling. However, if you were to put your money into a diversified stock portfolio, the gains made by other stocks in the portfolio would make up for the loss of one stock.

Diversification can include other asset classes like bonds, real estate, and commodities in addition to investing in various stocks or industries. To get the most out of each asset class's unique advantages and disadvantages, it's critical to have a well-diversified portfolio. You can mitigate market fluctuations over time and ensure that you are not overly exposed to any one risk by having a diverse portfolio.

Although the process of creating a diversified portfolio can be complicated, you can create a portfolio that is in line with your financial objectives and lowers your overall risk by following a few straightforward steps. A step-by-step guide to creating a diverse portfolio can be found here:

Identify your investment objectives: Identifying your investment objectives is the first step in creating a diversified portfolio. Understanding your risk tolerance, time horizon, and anticipated returns are all part of this.

Analyze your current financial circumstances: It is essential to evaluate your current financial situation before investing. This includes looking at your assets, debts, income, and expenses. This will assist you in determining the best investment vehicles and the amount of money you can afford to invest.

Select your asset types: The next step is to select the asset classes you want to incorporate into your portfolio. Stocks, bonds, real estate, and commodities are all examples of common asset classes. Diversifying your portfolio can lower your overall risk because each asset class has its own risk and return characteristics.

Determine how to divide your assets: Asset allocation is the next step after selecting your asset classes. This entails figuring out how much of your portfolio you want to be invested in each asset class. Your risk tolerance and investment objectives ought to be reflected in your asset allocation.

Put money into particular securities: You can begin investing in particular securities once you have established your asset allocation. Individual stocks, bonds, ETFs, and mutual funds are all included in this. Researching a security's risk, return, and growth potential is essential when selecting it.

Maintain a regular portfolio rebalance: Last but not least, it is essential to rebalance your portfolio regularly to keep your asset allocation in line with your investment objectives. To maintain your desired asset allocation, this may entail selling securities and reinvesting in other investments.

By minimizing overall risk and maximizing returns, a diversified portfolio can help you achieve your financial objectives. You can build a portfolio that meets your financial goals and gives you peace of mind by following these easy steps.

In conclusion, diversification is an essential idea in the investment industry. To minimize risk and maximize returns, this strategy involves diversifying your investments across various asset classes, industries, and geographical regions. A thorough financial analysis, a clear understanding of your investment goals, and careful selection of the asset classes you want to include are all necessary for creating a diversified portfolio. You can start investing in specific securities after determining your asset allocation, and you should regularly rebalance your portfolio to keep it in line with your objectives. You can build a portfolio that gives you peace of mind and achieve your financial goals if you follow these steps.

Chapter 6:

Understanding Market Cycles

The financial market is continually developing and changing, and it's fundamental to comprehend these progressions to go with informed venture choices. Market cycles allude to the regular high points and low points of the market, which are impacted by different economic, political, and mental variables. Understanding market cycles is critical for effective contributing because it assists you with settling on choices in light of the present status of the market, as opposed to being influenced by feelings or media melodrama.

There are a few kinds of market cycles, including economic cycles, bull markets, and bear markets. Economic cycles allude to the repetitive examples of economic development and constriction that happen after some time. During economic extension, organizations and shoppers will generally be hopeful and spend more cash, prompting expanded economic action and higher stock costs. On the other hand, during economic compressions, organizations and purchasers are warier in their spending, prompting discounted economic action and lower stock costs.

Bull markets and bear markets are terms used to depict the general pattern of the securities exchange. A bull market is a time of supported market development, described by rising stock costs and expanding financial backer certainty. Then again, a bear market is a time of supported market decline, described by falling stock costs and a general feeling of cynicism among financial backers.

To be a smart and safe investor, it is fundamental to understand how to perceive the various phases of the market cycle and go with informed choices in light of the ongoing market conditions. For instance, during a bull market, it very well might be a great opportunity to put resources into development stocks, while during a bear market, putting resources into guarded stocks or bonds might be more judicious.

It's likewise vital to remember that market cycles can be impacted by different variables, including loan fees, economic pointers, international occasions, and customer opinion. Hence, it's vital to watch out for the market and change your venture procedure on a case-by-case basis.

One more significant part of understanding market cycles is figuring out how to deal with your feelings during times of market unpredictability. At the point when stock costs are quickly rising or falling, it very well may be enticing to pursue hurried choices in light of feelings as opposed to reason. Notwithstanding, it's vital to remain trained and adhere to your money growth strategy, in any event, during market slumps.

In conclusion, understanding market cycles is an essential part of money management and an investment strategy. By perceiving the various phases of the market cycle and settling on informed choices given current market conditions, you can limit risk and boost returns. Watching out for market drifts and dealing with your feelings during times of unpredictability will likewise assist you with settling on sound speculation choices over the long haul.

Chapter 7:

The Power of Dividends &
Understanding Compound Intrest

Dividends are a form of payment made by a company to its shareholders, typically quarterly. They are a way for companies to return value to their investors, and they can provide a valuable source of income for those who invest in stocks. In this chapter, we'll explore the benefits of investing in stocks that pay dividends, and how they can play a role in your long-term investment strategy.

First, let's talk about the benefits of investing in dividend-paying stocks. One of the biggest advantages is that they can provide a stable source of income. Dividends can vary from quarter to quarter, but over time, they can provide a reliable stream of income for investors. This can be especially important for those who are approaching or in retirement, as it can help to supplement their income and provide a source of financial stability.

In addition to providing a source of income, investing in dividend-paying stocks can also help to reduce the overall volatility of your portfolio. This is because dividends can help to offset losses during market downturns, making your portfolio less sensitive to market fluctuations. This can provide a sense of stability and help you avoid making impulsive decisions during times of market uncertainty.

Another benefit of investing in dividend-paying stocks is that they can help you to build wealth over the long term. This is because, in addition to the dividends you receive, the value of the stocks you own can also increase over time. This increase in value, combined with the dividends you receive, can help you to build wealth and reach your financial goals.

It's also worth noting that investing in dividend-paying stocks can be a smart tax-saving strategy. In many countries, including the United States and Canada, dividends are taxed at a lower rate than other forms of investment income. This can help to reduce your overall tax bill, allowing you to keep more of your money to invest or spend as you see fit.

When it comes to investing in dividend-paying stocks, it's important to keep a few things in mind. Firstly, it's essential to do your research and find companies that have a strong track record of paying dividends. You should also look for companies that have a history of increasing their dividends over time, as this can indicate a healthy and growing business.

In conclusion, investing in dividend-paying stocks can be an effective way to generate a stable source of income, reduce the overall volatility of your portfolio, and build wealth over the long term. By doing your research and choosing high-quality companies, you can create a portfolio that provides both income and potential for capital appreciation. So, if you're looking to add some income-generating investments to your portfolio, consider investing in dividend-paying stocks.

One of the most powerful tools in investing is the concept of compound interest. Simply put, compound interest is the interest on a loan or deposit calculated based on both the initial principal and the accumulated interest from previous periods. This results in exponential growth over time, making it a crucial concept to understand for anyone looking to build their wealth through investment.

There are a few key things to keep in mind when using compound interest to build your wealth. Firstly, the longer the period, the greater the compound interest will be. This means it's essential to start saving and investing as early as possible. Secondly, the higher the interest rate, the faster your money will grow. This is why it's important to choose investments that offer high interest rates or have the potential for substantial capital appreciation.

Let's break down how compound interest works with a simple example. Imagine you have $1,000 that you invest at a 5% annual interest rate. After one year, you would have $1,050 (1,000 x 1.05 = 1,050). The next year, you would earn interest on the new total of $1,050, resulting in $1,102.50 (1,050 x 1.05 = 1,102.50).

See the table on the next page for more examples in a chart.

Year	Starting balance	Annual Interest	Ending Balance
1	$1000	$50.00	$1,050.00
2	$1,050.00	$52.50	$1,102.50
3	$1,102.50	$55.13	$1,157.63
4	$1,157.63	$57.88	$1,215.51
5	$1,215.51	$60.78	$1,276.29
6	$1,276.29	$63.81	$1,340.10
7	$1,340.10	$67.01	$1,407.11
8	$1,407.11	$70.36	$1,477.47
9	$1,477.47	$73.87	$1,551.34
10	$1,551.34	$77.57	$1,628.91
11	$1,628.91	$81.44	$1,710.35
12	$1,710.35	$85.52	$1,795.87
13	$1,795.87	$89.79	$1,885.66
14	$1,885.66	$94.28	$1,979.94
15	$1,979.94	$98.99	$2,078.93

Note: This is assuming a 5% annual interest rate.

As you can see, the more time that passes, the more exponential the growth becomes. This is why a long-term investment outlook is so important, we will talk more about the long-term outlook in a later chapter. By keeping your investments in place for an extended period, you give compound interest the time it needs to truly work its magic.

Rule of 72

Investing for the future is a common goal for many people, and it is important to have a solid understanding of the different concepts and tools available to help you reach your financial goals. One such tool is the rule of 72.

The rule of 72 is a simple calculation that helps you determine how long it will take for your money to double, based on a given interest rate. The formula is straightforward: simply divide 72 by the interest rate, and the answer will give you the number of years it will take for your investment to double.

For example, if you have $10,000 invested at an interest rate of 6%, it will take approximately 12 years for your investment to double ($10,000 x 2 = $20,000). This is because 72 divided by 6 equals 12, more in the table on the following page.

Interest Rate (%)	Years to Double (Using Rule of 72)
1	72
2	36
3	24
4	18
5	14.4
6	12
7	10.3
8	9
9	8
10	7.2

It is important to note that the rule of 72 is just an approximation and is based on the assumption that interest compounds annually. However, it is still a useful tool for understanding the impact of compound interest on your investments over time.

When planning your investment strategy, it is important to consider the length of time you want to invest and your expected return on investment. The rule of 72 can help you determine if your investment will reach your desired goals in a reasonable amount of time.

By incorporating the rule of 72 into your investment strategy, you can make informed decisions about your investments and work towards reaching your financial goals.

In conclusion, compound interest is a fundamental concept in investing that can lead to significant growth over time. By taking a long-term approach and carefully selecting investments with high interest rates, you can harness the power of compound interest to achieve your financial goals.

Chapter 8:

Understanding Taxes!

As an investor, it's important to understand the tax implications of your investment decisions. Everywhere has a different tax system, so it's crucial to understand the tax laws and regulations of the country where you are investing. This chapter will provide a basic overview of the tax considerations for investing in Canada and the United States.

Canada:
In Canada, all investment income, including dividends, interest, and capital gains, is subject to taxes. The tax rate for dividends depends on the province you reside in, while the tax rate for capital gains is 50% of your marginal tax rate. Additionally, registered retirement savings plans (RRSPs) and tax-free savings accounts (TFSAs) offer tax-deferred investment options. In an RRSP, investment income is taxed only when you withdraw it, while TFSAs allow you to earn investment income tax-free.

Canada also has several tax credits and deductions available to investors, such as the dividend tax credit, which reduces the tax payable on eligible dividends received from Canadian corporations. Additionally, investors may be eligible for the capital gains deduction, which reduces the tax payable on capital gains from the sale of qualified small business corporation shares.

United States:

In the United States, investment income is taxed as ordinary income, with tax rates ranging from 10% to 37% depending on your income bracket. Capital Gains from selling investments, such as stocks or real estate, are subject to capital gains tax, which is calculated based on the difference between the purchase price and sale price of the asset. Long-term capital gains, which are gains from assets held for more than a year, are generally taxed at a lower rate than short-term capital gains. The tax rate for long-term capital gains varies depending on the investor's income bracket but can range from 0% to 20%.

Additionally, investors in the United States may also be subject to state and local taxes on investment income. It is important to consult a tax professional or seek advice from the Internal Revenue Service (IRS) to understand the specific tax implications of your investment portfolio.

In summary, taxes can play a significant role in investment returns and should be considered as part of a comprehensive investment strategy. Investors in both Canada and the United States need to be aware of the tax implications of their investments and plan accordingly. It may be beneficial to seek advice from a financial advisor or tax professional to understand how to optimize your investment strategy and minimize your tax liability.

Chapter 9:

The Importance of a Long-Term Investment Outlook

Maintaining a long-term investment outlook is crucial to achieving success in the world of investing. Short-term market fluctuations can often be unpredictable and overwhelming, causing many investors to make impulsive decisions that can harm their investments in the long run.

Investing is a marathon, not a sprint, and having a long-term outlook allows investors to stay focused on their goals and not be swayed by short-term market movements. A long-term perspective helps to mitigate the impact of short-term volatility, reducing the risk of selling investments at a loss. This is because a long-term outlook allows investors to see beyond the ups and downs of the market and focus on the bigger picture.

One of the key benefits of having a long-term outlook is that it enables investors to take advantage of the power of compounding. Compounding is the process of earning interest on interest, and the longer the time horizon, the more powerful the compounding effect becomes. This means that investments that are held for longer periods have the potential to grow much larger than investments that are only held for short periods.

Additionally, having a long-term outlook helps to minimize taxes and transaction costs, as investors can avoid frequent buying and selling, which can generate significant taxes and fees over time. By taking a long-term approach, investors can reduce the impact of taxes and fees on their returns, allowing them to keep more of their investment gains.

In conclusion, a long-term investment outlook is essential for success in the world of investing. It enables investors to stay focused on their goals, take advantage of the power of compounding, and minimize the impact of taxes and fees. Investors who adopt a long-term perspective are more likely to achieve their financial goals and be successful in the long run.

Chapter 10:

A Simple Path to Long-Term Success with Index Funds

Investing in the stock market can be an intimidating process, but with the right strategy, it can also be a lucrative one. Index funds are an excellent investment option that can help simplify the process and achieve long-term success.

What are Index Funds?

Index funds are a type of mutual fund that aims to replicate the performance of a specific market index, such as the S&P 500. They are managed passively, meaning that the portfolio of stocks is not actively managed by a professional fund manager. Instead, the fund tracks the performance of the underlying index, and the composition of the portfolio is regularly adjusted to match the index's performance.

<u>**Advantages of Investing in Index Funds:**</u>

Diversification: Index funds provide broad exposure to a large number of stocks in different industries and sectors, reducing the overall risk in your investment portfolio.
Low Cost: Index funds have lower management fees than actively managed mutual funds, making them an excellent option for cost-conscious investors.
Historically Strong Performance: Over the long term, index funds have shown consistent and strong returns that often outperform actively managed mutual funds.

Ease of Use: Investing in an index fund is a straightforward process that can be done through a brokerage account, making it an accessible option for individuals who are new to investing.

<u>**Why Index Funds are a Good Option for the Average Investor:**</u>

Long-Term Performance: By investing in a broad market index, index funds offer the potential for long-term growth, which is crucial for building wealth over time.
Avoiding Market Timing: Trying to time the market and pick individual stocks can be a challenging

task, even for professional investors. By investing in an index fund, you avoid the need to try and predict market movements, and instead, rely on the overall performance of the market.

Ease of Management: Index funds are a low-maintenance investment option, requiring little to no effort on your part. This makes them an ideal option for those who want to invest for the long term without needing to constantly monitor their investments.

In conclusion, investing in index funds is a simple and effective way for the average person to participate in the stock market and achieve long-term financial success. With low costs, broad diversification, and strong historical performance, index funds offer a straightforward path to wealth-building that can be accessible to everyone.

Chapter 11:

Debt and Methods to Tackle It

Debt is a common issue that many people face, and it can be overwhelming to think about paying it off. However, with the right strategies, it is possible to manage debt effectively and improve your financial situation. In this chapter, we will discuss different methods for paying off debt, including credit card debt, and provide tips for reducing debt in the future.

Credit Card Debt

Credit card debt is one of the most common forms of debt and can quickly spiral out of control if not managed properly. To tackle credit card debt, it is important to focus on paying off the card with the highest interest rate first. This will help you save money on interest in the long run. Additionally, it can be helpful to transfer your balance to a card with a lower interest rate or to negotiate a lower rate with your credit card company.

Snowball Method

The snowball method is a debt repayment strategy that involves paying off your smallest debt first, then using the extra money you free up to tackle your next smallest debt. This method can be motivating because you see progress quickly, which can help keep you on track. As you pay off debts, you will have more money to put towards paying off the next debt.

Avalanche Method

The avalanche method is a debt repayment strategy that involves paying off the debt with the highest interest rate first. This method is more cost-effective in the long run because it will save you money on interest. However, it may take longer to see progress, which can make it less motivating.

Debt Consolidation

Debt consolidation is a strategy that involves taking out a loan to pay off multiple debts. This can simplify your debt repayment process by giving you one monthly payment to make instead of several. Debt consolidation loans often have lower interest rates, which can help you save money on interest over time.

Budgeting

Budgeting is one of the most important strategies
for managing debt. By tracking your spending and
creating a budget, you can ensure that you are
spending within your means and not adding to your
debt. It is also important to have an emergency fund
in place so that you are not relying on credit cards
in case of an unexpected expense.

In conclusion, managing debt takes time and effort,
but it is possible to get back on track with the right
strategies. Whether you choose to focus on paying
off the debt with the highest interest rate or the
smallest debt, it is important to stick to your plan
and make paying off debt a priority.

Chapter 12:

Navigating the Financial Services Industry

The financial services industry is a vast and complex landscape that can be overwhelming for many people, especially those who are just starting to invest. With so many options and conflicting advice, it's important to understand what you're looking for and how to evaluate different products and services. In this chapter, we'll cover some of the basics of understanding the financial services industry and offer some guidance on how to navigate it successfully.

Choosing a Financial Advisor

One of the biggest decisions you'll make as an investor is whether to work with a financial advisor. Financial advisors can help you create an investment strategy, manage your portfolio, and offer guidance on important financial decisions. But with so many advisors to choose from, how do you know which one is right for you?

The first step is to determine what type of advice you're looking for. Are you looking for someone to simply manage your investments, or do you need a comprehensive financial plan that covers your taxes, estate planning, and insurance needs? Once you know what type of advice you're looking for, you can start to research different advisors and compare their qualifications, fees, and services.

Another important factor to consider when choosing a financial advisor is their investment philosophy. Do they believe in active management or passive management? Do they have a track record of outperforming the market? These are important questions to ask, as your advisor's philosophy will have a significant impact on your portfolio's performance.

Evaluating Investment Products

With so many investment products to choose from, it can be difficult to know where to start. Some of the most common investment products include mutual funds, exchange-traded funds (ETFs), stocks, bonds, and annuities. Each type of product has its advantages and disadvantages, so it's important to understand what you're looking for and how each product fits into your overall investment strategy.

When evaluating an investment product, some of the key factors to consider include the product's investment objectives, fees, and historical performance. It's also important to understand the investment's underlying assets and the risks involved. For example, if you're considering a stock, you'll want to understand the company's financial health, competitive landscape, and future growth prospects.

Avoiding Scams and Fraud

Unfortunately, the financial services industry is not immune to scams and fraud. In recent years, there have been numerous high-profile cases of fraud in the investment world, and it's important to be aware of the warning signs so you can protect your hard-earned money.

One of the biggest red flags is an investment opportunity that promises unrealistic returns with little or no risk. If an investment seems too good to be true, it probably is. Another warning sign is high-pressure sales tactics or a lack of transparency about the investment's underlying assets and fees.

It's also important to be wary of unsolicited investment offers, especially if they come from someone you don't know. Before investing, always do your research and check the background of the investment and the advisor.

When it comes to investing, having the right broker can make all the difference. A good broker can help you reach your financial goals, offering access to a wide range of investment products, tools, and resources to make informed decisions. However, not all brokers are created equal. To maximize your returns and minimize your costs, it's important to choose a broker that aligns with your needs, values, and financial situation.

One of the key factors to consider when selecting a broker is cost. High fees can eat into your returns, so it's important to choose a broker that offers low or no fees. You can find brokers that offer low fees or commission-free trading, which can be a great option for those who are just starting to invest or those who prefer a more hands-on approach to managing their investments.

Another factor to consider is trust. You want to choose a broker that is reputable, well-established, and has a history of serving clients well. Look for brokers that are regulated by trusted financial organizations, such as the Financial Industry Regulatory Authority (FINRA) in the United States or the Investment Industry Regulatory Organization of Canada (IIROC) in Canada. These organizations ensure that brokers adhere to strict standards of conduct, and provide resources to investors who have concerns or questions about their investments.

In addition to cost and trust, you may also want to consider the type of investment products offered by the broker. Some brokers offer a wide range of investment products, while others specialize in a specific area, such as stock trading, bonds, or exchange-traded funds (ETFs). You'll want to choose a broker that offers products that align with your investment goals and strategy.

Finally, it's important to understand the level of service and support you'll receive from your broker. Look for brokers that provide resources and tools to help you make informed decisions, as well as educational materials, to help you understand the investment products and strategies you are considering. You may also want to consider working with a broker who has a strong reputation for customer service, and who is available to answer your questions and provide guidance when you need it.

In conclusion, understanding and navigating the financial services industry can be a complex task, but by taking the time to evaluate your options, understand your investment goals, and protect yourself from scams and fraud, you can be on your way to making informed and successful investment decisions, choosing the right broker is critical to achieving your financial goals. Take your time, do your research, and find a broker who aligns with your needs, values, and financial situation. Whether you are in the United States or Canada, there is a broker out there who can help you reach your financial goals and provide the low-cost, trusted support you need to grow your investments.

Chapter 13:

Understanding Inflation and Its Impact on Investments

Inflation is a key factor that can significantly impact your investments over time. Understanding what inflation is and how it works is crucial for anyone who wants to make informed investment decisions.

Inflation is the sustained increase in the general price level of goods and services in an economy over some time. This results in a decline in the purchasing power of money, meaning that the same amount of money will be able to buy fewer goods and services in the future.

Inflation is caused by a variety of factors, including:

1. Increase in demand for goods and services: When the demand for goods and services increases, it can drive up prices and lead to inflation.
2. Increase in production costs: When the costs of production, such as wages, raw materials, and energy, rise, it can lead to higher prices and inflation.

3. Expansion of money supply: An increase in the money supply, either through printing more money or through the growth of credit, can cause inflation.

4. Government policies: The government can also impact inflation through its fiscal and monetary policies. For example, increasing government spending can lead to inflation if not offset by other measures.

5. International trade: Changes in exchange rates and international trade can also impact inflation, especially in countries that are highly dependent on imports or exports.

6. Natural disasters and political instability: Natural disasters or political instability can disrupt the supply chain, causing prices to rise and leading to inflation.

7. Global pandemic: a global pandemic like COVID-19 is the more recent big event that led to a combination of supply chain issues, increased demand for items, and the expansion of money supply.

It's important to note that inflation can have both positive and negative effects on investments. On one hand, it erodes the purchasing power of money over time, making investments in stocks, bonds, and real estate more attractive. On the other hand, high inflation can lead to uncertainty and volatility in financial markets, making investment decisions more challenging.

Inflation can have a significant impact on your investments. It can erode the value of your investments, making it difficult to maintain your purchasing power. For example, if inflation is running at 3% per year, and your investments are only earning 2% per year, you are losing purchasing power each year. This is because the returns from your investments are not keeping up with the rise in prices.

To understand the impact of inflation on your investments, it's important to consider your investment time horizon and the rate of inflation. If you have a long-term investment horizon, you have more time to weather the effects of inflation. However, if you have a short-term investment horizon, you may need to consider investments that offer a higher return to compensate for the potential impact of inflation.

One of the key ways to manage the impact of inflation on your investments is to diversify your portfolio by investing in a range of assets that are less sensitive to inflation. This could include stocks, real estate, commodities, and other fixed-income investments.

It's also important to regularly monitor your investments and adjust your portfolio as necessary to ensure that it remains well-diversified and that you are positioned to weather the impact of inflation. This may involve rebalancing your portfolio regularly and adjusting your asset allocation to reflect changes in your investment goals, risk tolerance, and the economic environment.

In conclusion, understanding inflation and its impact on investments is critical for anyone looking to build a strong, well-diversified investment portfolio. By regularly monitoring your investments and adjusting your portfolio as needed, you can help ensure that your investments remain on track and that you are positioned to achieve your long-term investment goals.

Chapter 14:

Ethical Investing and ESG Considerations

In recent years, there has been a growing trend towards investing with a purpose. This involves considering not just the financial returns of an investment, but also its impact on the environment, society, and the governance of the companies being invested in. This type of investment philosophy is known as ethical investing or ESG (Environmental, Social, and Governance) investing.

ESG investing aims to align personal values with investment decisions. This means considering factors such as a company's environmental impact, labor practices, and diversity policies. By investing in companies that prioritize sustainability, social responsibility, and good governance, investors can support companies that share their values.

ESG investing is not only a matter of personal values but also a smart financial decision. Companies that prioritize ESG factors have been shown to have lower volatility, improved risk management, and better long-term financial performance compared to their peers. This is why

ESG investing has become increasingly popular in recent years, with the market for ESG-focused funds and ETFs growing rapidly.

For investors who are interested in ESG investing, there are a variety of investment options available.

These include:

- ESG-focused mutual funds and ETFs, which screen companies based on ESG criteria.
- SRI (Socially Responsible Investing) funds, which invest in companies that have a positive social and environmental impact.
- Impact investing invests in companies that actively work to solve specific social or environmental issues.

It's important to note that not all ESG funds and ETFs are created equal, and some may have higher fees and lower returns compared to traditional investments. As with any investment, it's important to thoroughly research and understand the ESG investment options before making a decision.

In conclusion, ethical investing and ESG considerations are important aspects of modern investment philosophy. By aligning personal values with investment decisions, investors can support

companies that share their values, while also
potentially benefiting from improved financial
performance.

Chapter 15:

Understanding Exchange-Traded Funds (ETFs)

Exchange-traded funds (ETFs) have become a popular investment option for many investors. In this chapter, we will explore what ETFs are and how they work, the benefits of investing in ETFs, and how to evaluate ETFs before investing.

What are ETFs?

ETFs are investment funds that are traded on a stock exchange, just like stocks. They are made up of a basket of securities, such as stocks, bonds, or commodities, and are designed to track the performance of a specific market index, such as the S&P 500. This allows investors to gain exposure to a wide range of assets with a single investment.

Benefits of Investing in ETFs

One of the biggest benefits of investing in ETFs is their versatility. They can be used to achieve a variety of investment objectives, including income generation, long-term growth, and diversification. ETFs are also a cost-effective way to invest, as they typically have lower management fees than actively managed funds. Additionally, because ETFs are traded on a stock exchange, they offer the flexibility of being able to buy and sell shares throughout the trading day.

Evaluating ETFs

When evaluating ETFs, there are several factors to consider. First, you should consider the expense ratio, which is the annual fee that the fund charges to cover its operating expenses. A lower expense ratio is generally better, as it means more of your investment returns are kept by you. You should also consider the tracking error, which is the difference between the performance of the ETF and the performance of the underlying index that it is tracking. A lower tracking error is generally desirable, as it means the ETF is closely tracking the performance of the index.

Another important consideration is the liquidity of the ETF, which refers to the ease with which you can buy or sell shares. ETFs that trade frequently and have a large number of shares outstanding are generally considered to be more liquid. You should also consider the diversification of the ETF, which refers to the number of different securities that are included in the fund. A more diversified ETF is generally less risky than one that is less diversified.

In conclusion, ETFs can be a useful tool for investors looking to achieve a variety of investment objectives. By understanding the basics of ETFs, the benefits of investing in ETFs, and how to evaluate ETFs, you can make informed investment decisions that can help you achieve your financial goals.

Chapter 16:

Building a Retirement Portfolio & Planning for Your Future

As you approach retirement, it's important to start thinking about how you'll finance your golden years. It is important to remember it's never too early to think about your retirement age and plan for when you're ready to retire. One of the best ways to secure your financial future is by building a retirement portfolio. A retirement portfolio is a collection of investments, such as stocks, bonds, and real estate, that are designed to provide a steady stream of income and growth to help you maintain your lifestyle in retirement. For me, I am setting myself up with my dividend investment portfolio and plan to retire hopefully in my 40's or 50's.

When building a retirement portfolio, it's important to consider a few key factors. First, it's important to think about your risk tolerance. This means considering how much volatility, or ups and downs, you're comfortable with in your investments. We discussed this in an earlier chapter, refer back for another look if you are still unsure. It's also important to think about your timeline, or how many years you have until you retire. The longer

your timeline, the more time you have to recover
from any short-term market fluctuations and build
up a larger portfolio. This is why it is so important
to start investing at a young age, we will talk about
this more in an upcoming chapter.

Next, it's important to consider asset allocation.
This means dividing your portfolio between
different types of assets, such as stocks, bonds, and
real estate, in a way that aligns with your risk
tolerance and investment goals. A well-diversified
portfolio can help to reduce your overall risk by
spreading your investments across multiple assets.

Another important factor to consider when building
a retirement portfolio is your income needs. This
means considering how much income you'll need in
retirement to maintain your desired lifestyle and
choosing investments that are likely to provide that
level of income. For example, bonds are typically a
more stable and income-generating investment,
while stocks offer the potential for higher growth
but can be more volatile.

Finally, it's important to regularly monitor your
retirement portfolio and make adjustments as
needed. This can help to ensure that your portfolio
stays aligned with your goals and risk tolerance and

that you're on track to reach your financial goals in retirement.

In conclusion, building a retirement portfolio is a critical component of planning for your financial future. By considering factors such as your risk tolerance, timeline, asset allocation, income needs, and regular monitoring, you can help build a retirement portfolio that meets your needs and helps you achieve your financial goals in retirement.

Chapter 17:

Building Generational Wealth

Legacy or generational wealth is the idea that an individual or a family's wealth is passed down from one generation to the next. This is one of my main goals when it comes to investing, I want to build something I can hand to my son and my son's kids. Building a legacy can be a powerful tool to create financial security, increase social mobility, and provide for future generations. However, creating generational wealth requires a long-term perspective and deliberate actions.

Unfortunately, many people do not have a culture of thinking long-term, and this can limit their ability to create intergenerational wealth. People often focus on short-term gains and immediate gratification rather than considering the long-term implications of their financial decisions. This approach may result in financial instability and missed opportunities to build wealth.

When you prioritize long-term thinking, you are more likely to make choices that will benefit you and your family for years to come. This can involve strategic investing, creating a robust retirement plan, and making thoughtful decisions about large purchases.

One way to build legacy wealth is to invest in assets that appreciate over time. For example, real estate, stocks, and bonds tend to increase in value over time, providing long-term wealth accumulation. Additionally, creating a family trust or establishing a family business can be an excellent way to pass down wealth from generation to generation. As you read earlier, Yugoslav is to get into real estate investing alongside my dividends.

It is essential to note that legacy wealth is not just about the money. It's also just as important to the values, behaviors, and skills that families pass down to future generations. By failing to properly teach education, discipline, and financial literacy you are limiting the amount of progress and potential growth you could achieve, those are only some of the key factors that contribute to creating intergenerational wealth. Ensuring that your children and grandchildren have a strong foundation in these areas can be just as important as building up a financial portfolio.

In conclusion, building generational wealth requires a long-term perspective, deliberate actions, and the development of strong financial habits. The benefits of creating a legacy extend beyond the financial realm and can provide a sense of security and purpose for future generations.

Chapter 18:

Not just a Ticker

When investing in the stock market, it's easy to get caught up in the excitement of buying and selling stocks. However, it's important to remember that when you buy a stock, you're not just buying a ticker symbol, but a share of a company. It's crucial to understand the company's fundamentals before deciding to invest.

Firstly, it's important to ask yourself what the company does. Is it in a sector that you understand and have knowledge of? Do you believe that the company's products or services have long-term potential? It's important to consider whether the company has a sustainable competitive advantage, which means that they have a unique offering that sets them apart from competitors and provides a barrier to entry for new players. A lot of people often forget that the company behind the ticker they are buying is a real company with real potential competitors, this can make it easier to lose money if you are just buying a stock ticker without doing your research.

Next, you should evaluate the company's financials to determine if it's profitable. Look at their revenue growth, earnings, and cash flow to determine whether the company is generating a positive return on investment. Also, consider the company's debt levels and whether they're sustainable. High levels of debt can indicate that the company is at risk of defaulting on its obligations, which could lead to financial distress.

Another important factor to consider is the strength of the management team. A good management team can make a significant difference in the success of a company. Look at their track record and experience, as well as their communication with shareholders. It's important to assess whether they're transparent and open with shareholders, as this can be an indication of the company's corporate governance practices.

When evaluating a company, it's also important to consider its long-term prospects. Is the company likely to be around for the next 20+ years? Are they providing a good or service that will be in demand in the long term? Look at trends in the industry and consider how the company fits into those trends. For example, if the company is in an industry that's likely to be disrupted by technology, it's important to consider how they're adapting to those changes.

In conclusion, when buying a share of a company, remember that it's more than just a stock. You're buying a slice of the company and its long-term prospects. By evaluating the company's fundamentals, including its products or services, financials, management, and long-term prospects, you can make a more informed decision about whether to invest. Always remember to do your research and consult with a financial advisor before making any investment decisions.

Chapter 19:

The Power of Starting Early

Investing is an essential part of securing your financial future, and time is your greatest ally in achieving your long-term goals. Starting early provides numerous benefits, including the power of compound interest that can turn even small contributions into significant sums over the long term. The earlier you start investing, the more time your money has to grow and the more potential it has to earn higher returns. I started investing in 2019-2020 but started to focus heavily on dividend investing at the end of 2021.

One significant advantage of starting early is that it allows you to weather market volatility and recover from any losses you may experience. When you have a longer investment horizon, you can afford to take on more risk and potentially earn higher returns over time. This flexibility can help you make sound investment decisions and avoid knee-jerk reactions to short-term market fluctuations like we've experienced in 2020 and again in 2023.

In addition to the financial benefits of investing, starting early also helps you establish good habits and a healthy mindset around money. Investing requires discipline, planning, and the ability to delay gratification - all of which are crucial skills that can translate to other areas of life. Starting early also gives you time to learn from your mistakes and adjust your investment strategy accordingly.

Many young people may feel like they don't have enough money to invest or that they have plenty of time to start later. However, even small contributions can make a big difference over time. Consider this: if you were to invest just $100 per month starting at age 25 with $0 invested and earn an average annual return of 7%, you would have around $250,000 by the time you reach age 65.

See table on the next page for more information.

Age	Years Invested	Total Invested	Estimated Value
25	0	$0	$0
30	5	$6,000	$8,368
35	10	$12,000	$19,497
40	15	$18,000	$32,220
45	20	$24,000	$48,056
50	25	$30,000	$68,122
55	30	$36,000	$94,853
60	35	$42,000	$131,410
65	40	$48,000	$250,341

Note: The estimated value is based on the assumption of a fixed monthly investment of $100 with a 7% average annual return, compounded annually, and does not take into account any taxes, fees, or other investment-related expenses. Actual returns may vary.

Of course, not everyone has the luxury of starting early, and there may be competing financial priorities like paying off debt or saving for emergencies. However, if you can make even a small investment in your future today, you'll thank yourself down the road. So, whether you're just starting your career or still in school, now is the time to start thinking about investing for the long term. Don't wait for a windfall or perfect timing - start small and stay committed. Your future self will thank you for it.

Chapter 20:

Protecting Yourself from Financial Scams and Fraud

Protecting Yourself from Financial Scams and Fraud

Investing your hard-earned money is a smart decision for your financial future, but it's crucial to be aware of the risks that come with it. Unfortunately, many scammers and fraudsters are waiting to take advantage of unsuspecting investors. In this chapter, we'll explore some of the most common financial scams and frauds and how you can protect yourself.

Types of Financial Scams and Fraud

Ponzi schemes: A Ponzi scheme is a type of investment scam in which returns are paid to earlier investors using the capital contributed by newer investors. The scheme eventually collapses when there aren't enough new investors to pay off the earlier ones.

Pyramid schemes: A pyramid scheme is similar to a Ponzi scheme, but it relies on recruiting new investors to make money, rather than investing in a legitimate business or investment opportunity.

Pump-and-dump schemes: In a pump-and-dump scheme, a group of fraudsters artificially inflate the price of a stock by spreading false or misleading information about the company. Once the price has risen, they sell their shares, leaving other investors with losses.

Advance-fee scams: Advance-fee scams involve convincing investors to pay a fee upfront in exchange for a promise of a larger payout later. However, the promised payout never materializes, and the investor loses their money.

Identity theft: Identity theft involves stealing someone's personal information to access their financial accounts or make fraudulent purchases.

Protecting Yourself from Financial Scams and Fraud

Do your research: Before investing in any opportunity, do your due diligence and research the company and investment thoroughly. Check the company's financial statements, business practices, and history.

One of the best ways to protect yourself from financial scams and fraud is to do your research before investing your money. It's important to thoroughly investigate any investment opportunity that comes your way, even if it seems legitimate at first glance. Doing your research can help you identify any red flags that may indicate a potential scam or fraud.

Start by researching the company or investment in question. Look for information about the company's financial statements, business practices, and history. You can find this information on the company's website or through reputable financial news sources. Be wary of any investment opportunity that doesn't provide this information or is hesitant to share it with you.

Another important aspect of research is to look for reviews and opinions from other investors. Check online forums, social media groups, and investment websites for feedback and opinions about the investment in question. Keep in mind that not all opinions may be reliable, so it's important to weigh the pros and cons of each investment opportunity carefully.

Be skeptical of unsolicited offers: If you receive an unsolicited investment offer, be cautious. Legitimate investment opportunities are typically not offered to strangers.

Another way to protect yourself from financial scams and fraud is to be skeptical of any unsolicited investment offers. These offers may come in the form of an email, phone call, or even a letter in the mail. While some legitimate investment opportunities may be offered in this way, it's important to be cautious and do your research before investing any money.

One common unsolicited investment offer is the "hot tip." This is when someone claims to have insider knowledge about a stock or investment that is sure to make you money. However, these tips are often based on rumors or false information and can lead to significant losses.

If you receive an unsolicited investment offer, take the time to research the company or investment thoroughly before making any decisions. Don't be pressured into making a quick decision, and don't provide any personal information or payment until you're sure the opportunity is legitimate.

Watch for red flags: Be wary of any red flags that may indicate a potential scam or fraud. Some common red flags include:

- Promises of high returns with little to no risk
- Pressure to invest quickly
- Offers of exclusive access to an investment opportunity
- Requests for personal information or payment upfront
- Lack of transparency or information about the investment opportunity

If you notice any of these red flags, it's important to proceed with caution and do your research before investing any money. Remember that if an investment opportunity seems too good to be true, it probably is.

Use a reputable broker: For example, I currently use WealthSimple for investing. When investing in the stock market, it's important to use a reputable broker who is licensed and regulated by the appropriate authorities.
One of the best ways to protect yourself from financial scams and fraud is to use a reputable broker when investing in the stock market. A reputable broker should be licensed and regulated

by the appropriate authorities and should have a good reputation in the industry.

Before choosing a broker, do your research and compare different options. Look for a broker with a good track record, reasonable fees, and a user-friendly platform. Check reviews and opinions from other investors to get a sense of their experience with the broker.

Protect your personal information: Identity theft is a common form of financial fraud, so it's important to protect your personal information at all times. Protecting your personal information is another important way to protect yourself from financial scams and fraud. This includes your social security number, bank account information, and investment account information.

Be wary of any requests for personal information, especially from someone you don't know or trust. Never provide your personal information over the phone or email, and be cautious when entering it online.

It's also a good idea to monitor your credit report regularly to ensure that no one has opened accounts in your name without your knowledge.

In conclusion, protecting yourself from financial scams and fraud is essential when investing your money. By doing your research, being skeptical of unsolicited offers, watching for red flags, using a reputable broker, and protecting your personal information, you can reduce your risk of falling victim to financial fraud. Remember to always proceed with caution and trust your instincts when it comes to investing your money.

<u>Closing Thoughts</u>

As we conclude this remarkable voyage through the intricacies of investing and the world of finances, my heart is filled with immense gratitude towards you, our valued readers. Thank you for embarking on this journey alongside me. Throughout these pages, we've explored the principles of financial growth, risk management, and wealth building. I trust that you've unearthed invaluable knowledge that will serve as a compass for your financial decisions. In your pursuit of financial security and prosperity, always remember that learning is a lifelong adventure. The financial landscape continually evolves, presenting new opportunities and challenges. Embrace these changes with curiosity and adaptability. As you close this chapter, my sincerest wish is that you carry forward not just the lessons learned but also the sense of empowerment and confidence to navigate the complex world of finance. Your financial journey is unique, and you have the tools to make it a success. I extend my heartfelt appreciation for being a part of this voyage. Your commitment to enhancing your financial literacy is a testament to your dedication to a brighter financial future for yourself and those you care about. In closing, I want to remind you that your financial well-being is not just about numbers on a balance sheet; it's about the choices you make and the life you envision. May your financial decisions align with your dreams and aspirations. Thank you once again for your trust and engagement. I look forward to seeing you on the shores of financial success. Here's to your ongoing financial adventure!